This book belongs to

WALT DISNEY
VOLUME 11

ALL ABOUT YOU

WALT DISNEY FUN-TO-LEARN LIBRARY

ISBN 1-885222-02-5
Advance Publishers Inc., P.O. Box 2607, Winter Park, FL. 32790
Printed in the United States of America
0987654321

Do you ever think about all of the things you do each day that keep you busy and make you happy? Did you know that even when you are asleep you are busy doing things? There is so much you can find out about yourself, and about how to take care of yourself, too. It's very exciting, learning all about *you*.

When you were born, you were a very little baby. You couldn't walk or talk or play or do any of the things that you do now. Think how much bigger you are, now that you have grown. All the time you are busy playing and learning, you are also growing. You will keep getting bigger and bigger until you are about 18 years old. After that you will stop getting taller, but you might still get fatter.

But you need something to keep you growing and playing and learning. Do you know what it is?

It's the food you eat. Food makes you grow, and it gives you energy. Energy helps you do things you want to do, like running and jumping and playing. Your body makes energy out of food. But you need good food—like meat and bread and vegetables and fruit and milk and cheese. Candy and cakes don't give you the right kind of energy to help you grow up strong and healthy.

When you eat, you chew the food with your teeth, and break it into little pieces. Then you swallow, and the food goes down into your stomach. Your stomach digests it by squeezing it into tiny pieces. Once it is digested, the food that makes you grow and gives you energy goes to all the parts of your body.

Your bones hold up your body. All your bones together are called your skeleton. You have big bones and small bones inside of you. The biggest are your arm bones and leg bones. The smallest are in your hands and feet. You even have three tiny bones in each ear. Your bones protect the soft inside parts of you, like your heart and lungs.

Your bones are very hard. Because they are hard, they can't bend. But there are places called joints where two bones meet, and luckily, joints can bend. Your elbows, knees, hips, shoulders, wrists, and ankles are all joints.

Your muscles hold you together and help you move. Muscles are like thick ropes attached to your bones. You use your muscles when you move your arms or your legs. When you want to bend your arm, your muscles get shorter and bunch up. When you want to put your arm down again, your muscles get longer—and down goes your arm.

Your heart is a muscle that is about the size of your closed fist. It squeezes hard and pushes your blood all through your body. Each time your heart squeezes, it makes a little thump inside your chest. You can feel it if you put your hand against your chest. This thump is called your heartbeat.

Your heart beats all the time, even when you are asleep. It usually beats 70 to 80 times a minute. But if you run very hard, it will beat faster.

You also breathe in and out all the time. When you breathe in, your lungs take in big gulps of air. A part of this air is called oxygen. Oxygen is very important because people must have oxygen to live.

Your lungs are like two bags inside your chest. As you breathe in, these bags fill up with air. The oxygen in the air passes through your lungs and is carried to every part of your body. When you breathe out, the part of the air your body doesn't need goes back out of your mouth and your nose.

You usually breathe in and out about 18 times a minute. But if you are running or playing hard, you use up more oxygen, so you need to breathe faster. That's why you start to get out of breath when you run very fast. When you are sleeping or resting, you breathe more slowly.

Your skin is your outside covering. It's waterproof, and it protects you from germs. If you get a cut, your skin makes a little scab to cover the cut while it is healing. Then germs can't get inside. A scab is your own homemade bandage.

Skin comes in many different colors, but everyone is some shade of brown—from very light brown to very dark brown. It depends on how much brown color, or pigment, you have in your skin. The freckles on your nose—or all over you—are also little clumps of brown coloring.

So no one is as white as snow, or as black as night. And what someone is like inside has nothing to do with the color of that person's skin.

Hair, too, comes in different colors. The thick hair on your head protects your head from the sun in the summer and the cold in the winter. Although sometimes, you need to wear a warm hat, as well.

You have hair all over your body as well as on your head.
This hair is very fine and short, not like the long hair covering
dogs and cats. It, too, protects you from the sun, and warms you
up in winter.

Your eyelashes and eyebrows shade and protect your eyes.
So, you can see that hair helps quite a lot.

Your hands are another very important part of you. Think of the many things you do with your hands. You paint pictures with your hands. You eat with your hands. You even count with your hands (using your fingers, of course). People make all kinds of things with their hands, although sometimes, that's not so easy to do!

And what about your feet—the parts of you that carry you around all day? Every time you take a step, your toes make a little grab at the ground and keep you from falling. Some people can even pick up things with their toes, but you may have noticed that hands are much better for that.

Aren't you glad you have teeth to chew your food with? If you couldn't use your teeth to chew your food, your poor stomach wouldn't be able to digest all those big lumps.

Your first set of teeth are called your baby teeth. When you are about six years old, these teeth begin to fall out. Underneath your baby teeth is a whole set of other teeth — your grown-up teeth. Take good care of these teeth, they have to last you the rest of your life.

Teeth are bones covered with enamel. That makes them very hard. But sometimes your teeth get little holes in them, called cavities. This may happen when you don't brush them. The old food stays on your teeth, making the enamel wear away, or decay. The dentist can clean your teeth and fill the cavities.

Inside your head is a very important part of you called your brain. All your thinking is done there. But your brain does much more than help you think. It takes care of you in other ways, even though you may not know that anything is happening. Your brain keeps your heart beating, your stomach digesting, and your lungs breathing in and out all the time. Your brain never sleeps, although parts of it do rest while you sleep.

Your brain is also like a big closet. It stores up everything you do and learn, so that you can remember it all later.

You have some very important helpers called your senses. You have five senses—sight, hearing, smell, taste, and touch.

You see with your eyes. You can see things up close, like flowers and bugs, and you can see things far away, like clouds and stars.

Your eye is like a little round camera that makes a picture of what you see and sends it to your brain. When your eyes are open, the light that bounces off things goes into your eyes and makes the picture. When your eyes are closed, there is no light shining into them, and you can't see.

Shut your eyes tight. Now open them again. What can you see?

You hear with your ears. When something makes a noise, it sends waves of sound through the air. These waves make your eardrums quiver—the way the top of a drum quivers when you hit it.

Sometimes, things make such loud sounds that you have to put your hands over your ears. Or sometimes, you have to listen very carefully to find out what is going on.

When you hear something, you must also figure out the sound that you are hearing. Is it a clock ticking? Is it a dog barking? Is it your mother calling you for supper?

Your nose is good for two things. You breathe in and out through your nose, and you smell things with your nose. When air goes into your nose, your nose picks up all the different smells that are around you — like flowers or delicious food. Those are good smells. But not all smells are good. You can always hold your nose if you don't like the smell of something.

Your sense of smell also helps you enjoy the food you are eating. Nothing tastes good when you have a cold, because you can't smell with your nose all stuffed up.

You taste things with your tongue. Your tongue is covered with tiny bumps called taste buds. The taste buds on different parts of your tongue help you recognize different tastes. The front ones taste sweet things and salty things. The side ones taste sour things like lemons and pickles. The back ones taste bitter things.

You might wish you could taste only the things you like, not those you don't like. Of course, some things taste bad because you are not supposed to eat them. But sometimes, you just don't like the way something tastes. And once in a while, the oddest things taste great!

Touch is another one of your senses. When your skin touches something, you can tell many things about it. It might be wet. It might be dry. It might be rough, or it might be smooth. Some things are hot, and some are cold. And some are soft, or hard, or sharp.

If you pet a cat, you can feel how soft and smooth it is. If you pick up a stone, you can tell whether it is dry, or wet, or rough, or smooth. You can also tell the shape of something when you feel it with your hands.

Sometimes it is not a good idea to touch something. If you
start to pick up a pan, and the pan is too hot, your skin tells you,
"That's too hot, put that down!" You also probably say "OUCH!"

Do you know what happens when your body needs something? When you are hungry, your stomach growls. It is saying, "Feed me." If you never felt hungry, you would probably forget to eat.

When you need water, you feel thirsty. Then you run to get a glass of water.

When you are cold, your skin gets little goose bumps, and you start to shiver. That warms you up. You also put your thick sweater on.

Because you have so many things to do all day, you get very tired. That's why you feel sleepy at night. Everyone needs sleep. Since you are young and still growing, you need even more sleep than your mother and father. Growing takes a lot of energy. While you are asleep, your heart keeps beating and your lungs keep breathing. You are also busy having dreams.

Your body has special ways to let you know if things are all right inside. One way is pain. You probably wish you didn't have to feel hurt, but pain is a way of telling you that you need to take care of something. Otherwise, you might not know that anything is wrong. If your eye hurts, the pain may be telling you that something is in your eye. If your shoes are uncomfortable, your feet begin to hurt. Your feet are telling you, "Take those off!" So you do.

Sometimes, you don't feel well. You may even have a fever. Then your mother takes your temperature and sends you to bed. A fever is one way that your body has to fight off germs. If you rest, you can use all your energy to fight those germs — and win.

Sometimes, you are so sick you have to see a doctor. But a doctor isn't someone you see only if you are sick. When you go to the doctor and have a checkup, the doctor weighs you and measures you to see how much you've grown since the last visit. The doctor checks your ears, looks down your throat, and looks into your eyes.

The doctor might also give you an injection. Some people call it a "shot." It feels like a very short, big pinch. Injections help your body fight off germs. They do hurt a little, but being sick feels worse, and lasts much longer than a little injection.

People have other kinds of feelings beside feeling sick or sleepy or hungry. Often you feel happy. And sometimes you feel angry or sad or lonely or frightened.

Everyone has these feelings inside them at one time or another. They are part of what makes you yourself.

Sometimes you get angry when you make a mistake. Other times you are sad because something is wrong, or you don't understand something. Even your friends may not understand how badly you feel. But if you talk to someone, often that person can make you feel better. This is one way that people help each other.

At the end of the day, it's
time to brush your teeth,
wash your face, comb your hair

— and get ready for bed. After all, your body needs plenty of rest to do some exciting things tomorrow. And the more good things you do for yourself, the more good things *you* can do.